ILLUSTRATED ENCYCLOPEDIA
HUMAN BODY

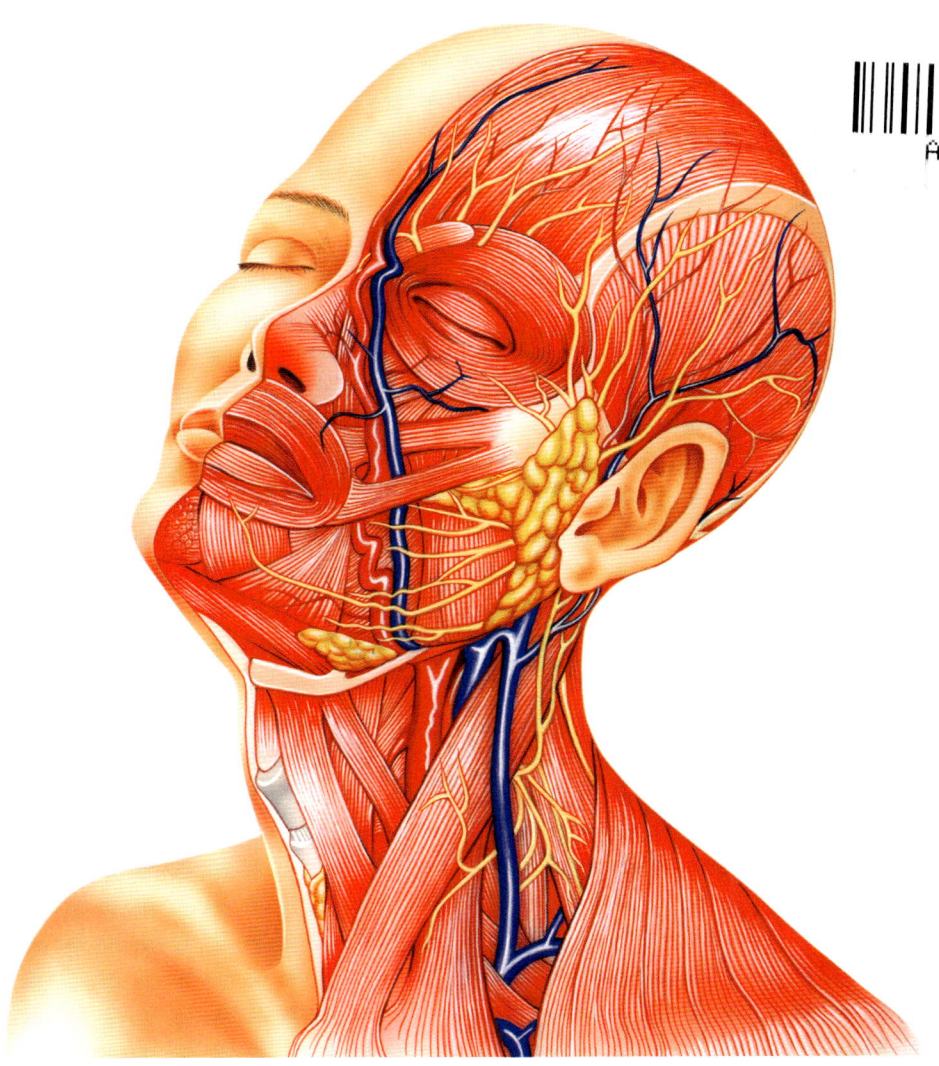

Managing Editor: Dr. Geeta Rani Arora
Editor: Ms. Pawanpreet Kaur
Education Consultant: Dr. Bimla Arora, *Shemrock School*
Copyright © with the publisher

Pegasus
An imprint of
B. Jain Publishers (P) Ltd.
USA - EUROPE - INDIA

HUMAN BODY

Organs and Parts

Human body is made up of many parts and organs. Every body part and organ has its own special job. All the parts function together to make the body run smoothly. Energy to run the body smoothly comes from the food and oxygen we take in.

Body Systems

Human body has a complex set up. There are eleven body systems that run the body effectively. They are circulatory system, respiratory system, immune system, skeletal system, muscular system, excretory system, endocrine system, digestive system, reproductive system, integumentary system, and nervous system. All body systems function in coordination with each other.

Food and Nutrition

We can keep ourselves in good health with the help of the food we eat. Eating right food in correct amount fulfils all the nutritional requirements important for the growth of our body. Eating balanced diet regularly helps in maintaining our health and preventing us from falling sick. A balanced diet contains all the nutrients in correct amount.

Quick Look
Running, cycling, and jumping rope are high intensity exercises to improve stamina.

The human body is built on a bony framework and comprises the organs, blood vessels, nerves, and muscles.

Swimming makes muscles stronger and provides strength.

Carbohydrates, proteins, fats, vitamins, minerals and water are essential nutrients required for body growth.

Human Body

Nutrients and Their Sources

Nutrient	Function	Sources
Carbohydrate	energy giving nutrient	common sugar, fruits, milk, vegetables such as potatoes, beans and rice.
Protein	body-building nutrient	milk and meat products, wheat, corn, rice, beans
Fats	energy storing nutrient	vegetable oils, butter, cheese, eggs, and animal fat
Vitamins and Minerals	protective and regulatory nutrients	fruits and vegetables, milk and meat
Water	dissolves and transports other nutrients and regulates body temperature	

Stages of Life

Infancy - the first and the youngest stage of a human being is infancy. An infant cannot speak and walk but can express his emotions by crying, smiling or moving hands and legs.

Childhood - the stage between infancy and adolescence is childhood. A child learns to walk, speak, and think about his surroundings and culture.

Adolescence - At this stage, various biological changes like development of sexual organs and psychological changes occur.

Adulthood – after the age of 18, an adolescent becomes an adult. He becomes physically and socially mature and emotionally strong.

Aging

When we become older, it is called ageing. Our body systems become less efficient and cannot function properly. This leads to various disorders and diseases, and body becomes weak due to diseases.

A baby remains an infant until one year of age.

The major consequences of aging are poor eyesight, skin wrinkles, and low blood circulation leading to low energy levels.

HUMAN BODY

Cells

Cells are the smallest functional units of all living organisms. They are the building blocks of human body. Cells can only be seen through a microscope. Many organisms are unicellular and others are multicellular.

Cell Structure

Cell membrane, cytoplasm, and nucleus are the three main parts of a cell. Nucleus is the control centre of a cell. It carries the information necessary for cell functions. The cell membrane entirely covers the cell. Cytoplasm is the gel-like fluid inside the cell that contains the cell organelles.

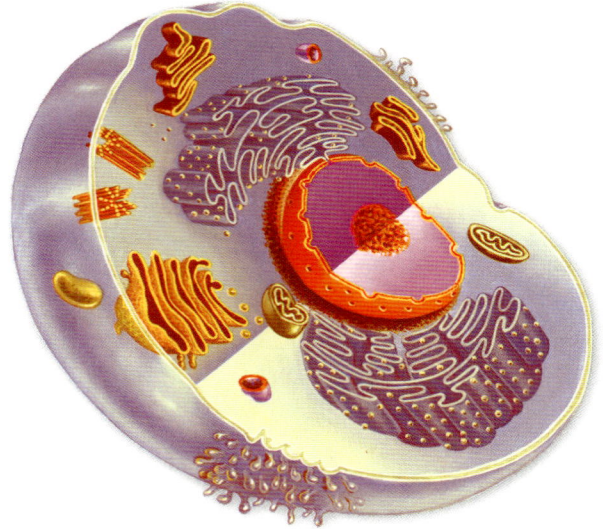

Cell organelles are the basic components of a cell that perform various functions inside the cell.

Cell Division

The process of multiplication of cells is called cell division. Through the process of cell division, millions of new cells are daily produced in our body that replace old and dying cells. Mitosis and meiosis are the two types of cell division. Cells multiply and form new ones by mitosis for our body system to work. Meiosis produces sex cells that give birth to new human beings.

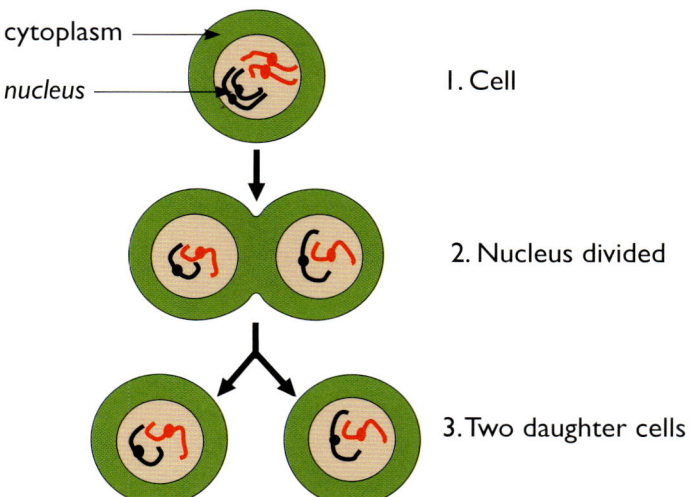

1. Cell
2. Nucleus divided
3. Two daughter cells

Cytokinesis is the division of cytoplasm and karyokinesis is the division of a cell's nucleus to form daughter cells.

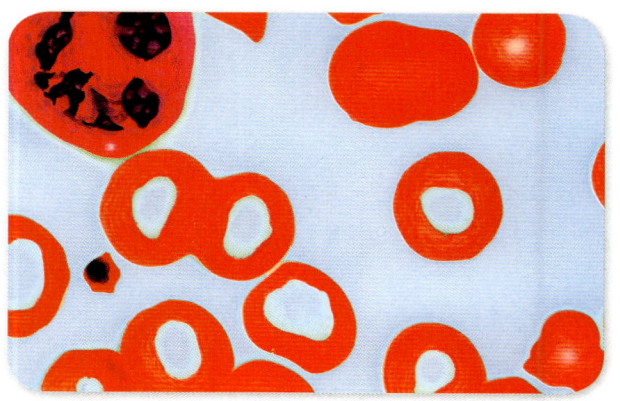

Red blood cells

Types of Cells

Different types of cells constitute the body systems. For example, nerve cells make the nervous system. Blood is composed of red blood cells and white blood cells. Cells also differ in shape and size. For example, nerve cells are long, thin and narrow, while muscle cells are rod-shaped.

4

Cells, Tissues and Organs

Tissues

Tissues are a group of similar cells that perform a specialised task. The main functions of tissues are to provide insulation, store fat and energy and help in motion and posture. Tissues cover the body and surfaces of organ and line internal spaces.

Types of Tissues

Epithelial tissue, connective tissue, muscle tissue and nerve tissue are the types of tissues. Epithelial tissues cover the whole surface of the body and provide a lining to all internal organs, body cavities and hollow organs. Connective tissues add support and structure to the body. Muscle tissues provide movement to our body. Nervous tissues coordinate and control various body activities.

Organs

Cells group to form tissues and tissues group to form organs. Organs are the main components of human body that perform specific tasks. Many organs such as the brain and the kidneys carry out multiple tasks. Groups of related organs form organ systems.

Quick Look

Although all cells differ in size, shape and function, the basic components of all cells are the same.

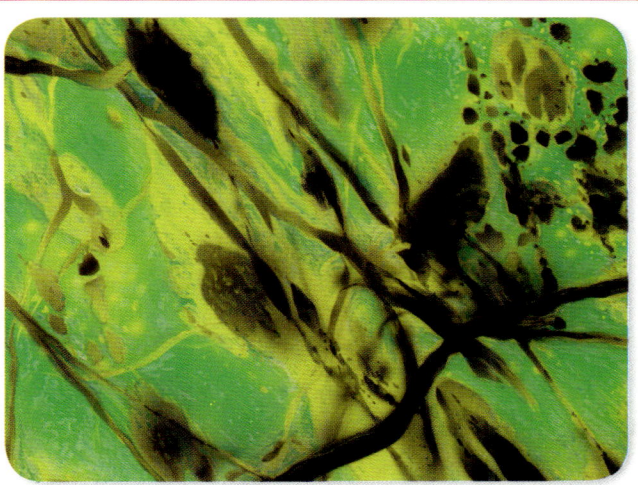
Tendons, ligaments, cartilage, bone, blood are examples of connective tissues.

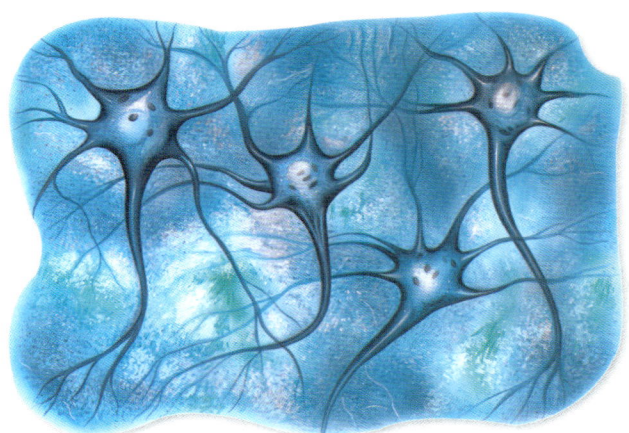
A network of nerve tissues.

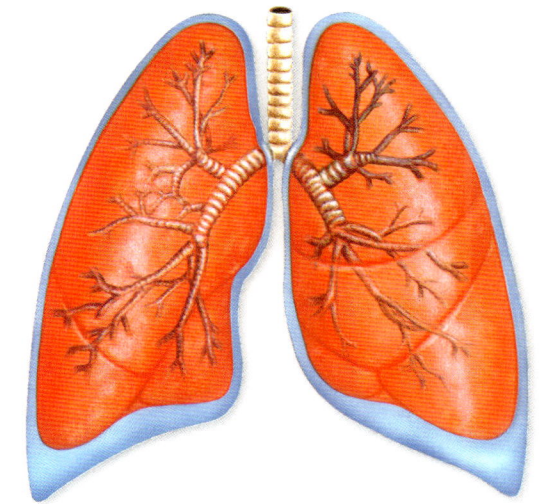
Lungs are one of the major organs that pump oxygen and carbon di-oxide in and out of our body.

HUMAN BODY

Eyes

Eyes are our seeing organs. Each eye is about 2.5 centimeters in length and weighs about 7 grams. Eyes capture images of objects and surroundings and help us to see. Conjunctiva, a clear mucus membrane protects eyes and keeps them moist.

Layers of Eyes

Sclera is the outermost, tough tissue layer that protects the eyes. It attaches to the cornea, the front surface of eye. Choroid is the next layer to cornea that contains blood vessels. Retina is the innermost layer that contains millions of light sensitive cells.

How do we see?

Light enters the eye through cornea, the outermost part of eye. The light then passes through iris – a coloured membrane. Pupil is the center of iris. Light then hits the lens after passing through the pupil. The lens focuses the light on to the retina and forms clear, sharp images. The sensitive cells in the retina send these image signals to the brain. Brain receives these signals and converts them into the images we see.

Rods and Cones

Rods and cones are special cells present in the retina. There are about 120 million rods and 7 million cones in each eye. The rod cells help us in differentiating between the shapes of objects.

Eye colours in human beings range from black to brown to blue or green.

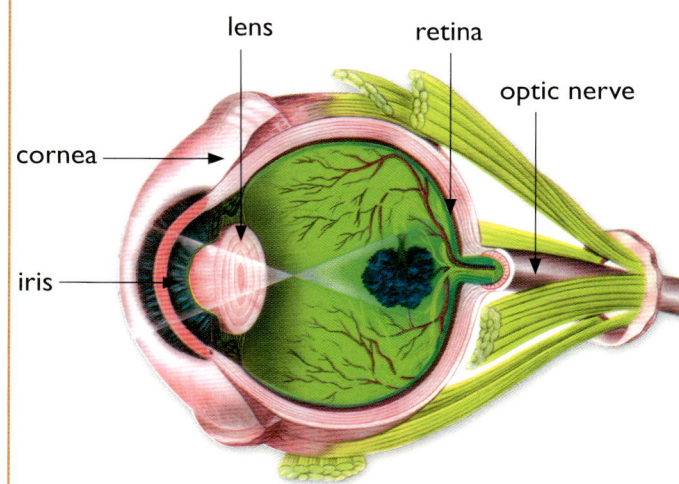

Optic nerve carries image signals to the brain.

Cone cells in the eye help us to distinguish colours.

Eyes and Ears

Tear

There are special glands called lachrymal glands behind the outer part of each upper lid. They produce tears that flow into the eyes from the glands through tiny tear ducts.

Ears

Ears are organs that help us to hear. Outer ear, middle ear and inner ear are three basic parts of an ear. The outer ear (pinna or auricle) is the visible, external part of the ear. The middle ear is an air-filled cavity that has ossicles. The ossicles convert sound waves into vibrations. The eardrum separates the middle ear from the external ear. The inner ear consists of the cochlea, a small, curled tube filled with liquid and tiny hair. The liquid and hair are set into motion when the ossicles in the middle ear vibrate.

How do we hear?

Sound waves travel in air. The outer ear catches and collects these sound waves and sends to the middle ear through the ear canal. The eardrum converts these waves into vibrations, which pass through three tiny bones in the middle ear and travel to the cochlea in the inner ear. The fluid and tiny hair present in the cochlea vibrate and send the sound signals to the brain thus we can hear.

Quick Look

Myopia is an eye disorder that results in the inability to see distant objects clearly.

Crying is the process of shedding tears.

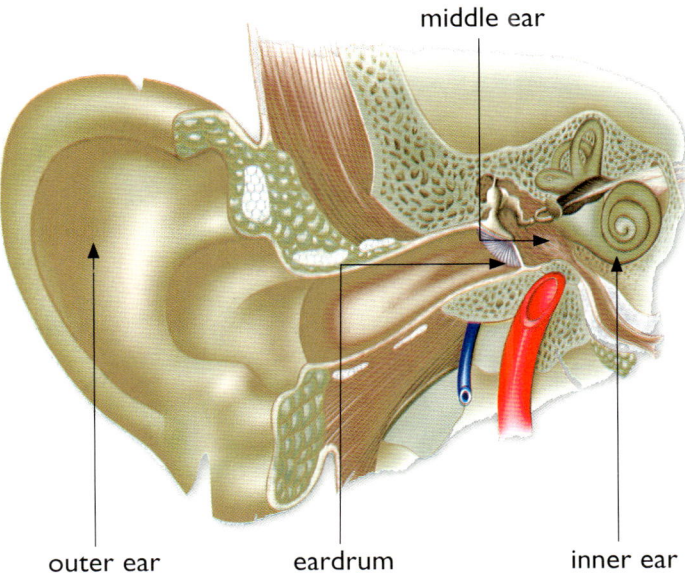

The ossicles, in the middle ear—malleus, incus and stapes—are the tiniest bones in the body.

Earwax

Our ear has sebaceous glands that secrete a substance called earwax. Earwax helps clean the ear canal, keeps dirt out of the ear, and lubricates the skin in the ear. It also protects the ears from infections.

HUMAN BODY

Nose

Nose is the organ of smell and also an organ of the respiratory system. The tiny nerve cells inside the nose help us to smell. Nostrils are the external openings to the nose, which are separated by a wall called septum.

How do we smell?

There are different odour particles produced by food, perfumes, etc. in the air that enter our nose through the nostrils. After entering through the nostrils, they reach the nasal cavity. The roof of the nasal cavity contains tiny nerve cells that send smell signals to the brain and help us sense all kinds of smells.

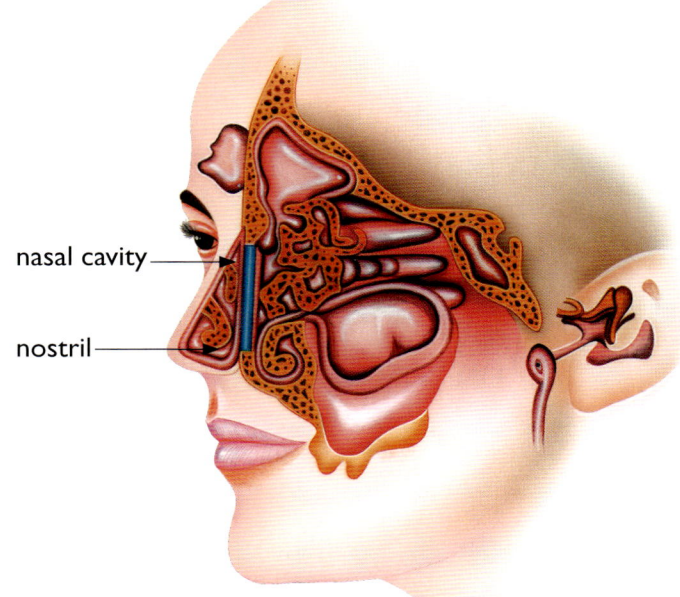

Nose is made up of bones and cartilages.

Mouth

Mouth is the opening, mainly responsible for taking in food and delivering speech. The tongue in the mouth tastes the food, teeth chew the food and the salivary glands lubricate the food and help in swallowing it. Palate is the roof of the mouth.

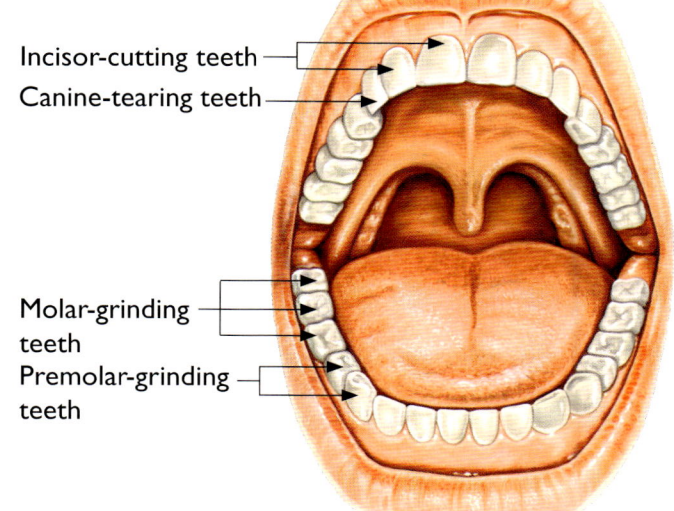

Incisors, canines, molars and premolars are the four types of teeth.

The air we inhale is warmed, filtered and moistened by the nose and then sent to the lungs through the windpipe.

Teeth Sets

Primary teeth are the first set of teeth of a child that grow at the age of three. The primary set consists of 20 teeth. The permanent set grows by the age of six and replaces primary teeth as they fall. The set of 28 permanent teeth appears by the age of 12 or 13. The set of 32 teeth completes in adulthood.

Nose and Mouth

Teeth

Teeth are white, bony structures that grow inside the mouth and help to chew and crush the food we eat. Teeth are fixed to the jawbone at the root and the part we see is the crown. Enamel covers the crown and protects the inside of the tooth. Below the enamel, lies the dentine that protects the pulp or soft part of the tooth. Pulp contains the nerve endings and the blood vessels.

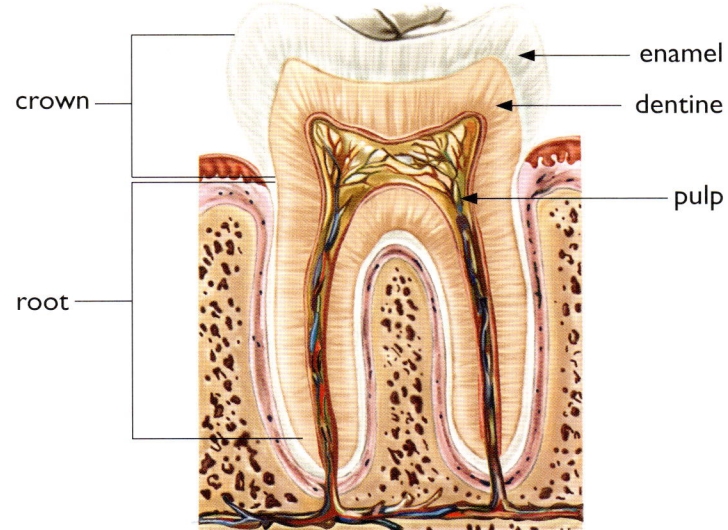

Enamel is the hardest substance in the human body.

Tongue

Tongue is the tasting organ of our body. Tongue has tiny taste buds on its surface that helps it to detect different tastes. There are about 10,000 taste buds on our tongue. Tongue also helps us in talking, chewing, swallowing and singing.

Quick Look

Nose also helps in tasting food, it makes us enjoy the food better as it helps us relish it with its aroma. If we have a cold or a blocked nose, the food we eat will not taste as good as it is.

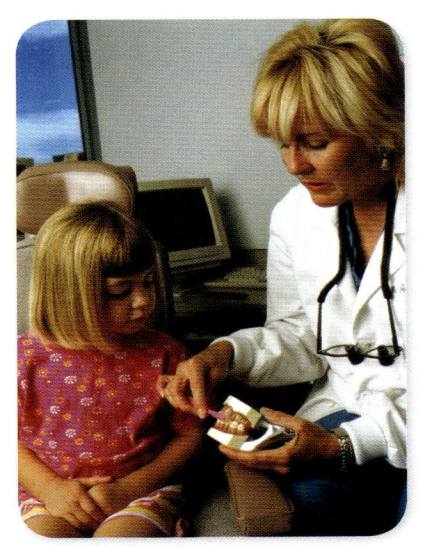

A dentist showing a child how to brush her teeth correctly.

Taste Buds

There are different groups of taste buds that sense sweet, bitter, sour, and salty tastes. Each taste bud has cells with tiny, sensitive nerve fibers. When we eat something, these fibers send messages to the brain and the brain identifies the taste for us.

A decrease in ability to taste is called hypogeusia and a total loss of taste is called ageusia.

HUMAN BODY

Skin

Skin is our body's external covering and is the largest organ of the body. The skin protects our body from the environment, particularly the sun. It also prevents excessive water loss from the body, regulates body temperature and protects the body from infection.

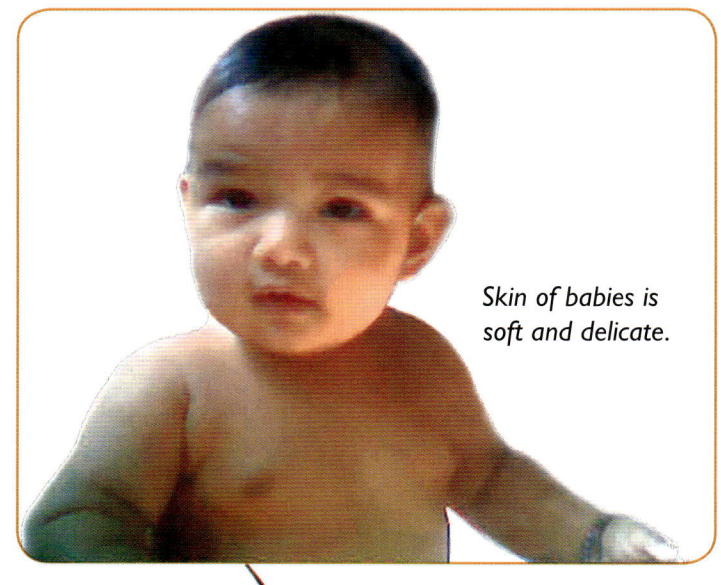
Skin of babies is soft and delicate.

Skin Layers

Our skin is made of three layers: epidermis, dermis and hypodermis. The epidermis is the outermost protective layer. The dermis contains nerves, blood vessels, hair follicles, glands and sensory receptors. The hypodermis is a fatty layer that acts as an energy reserve and also helps the body stay warm.

Quick Look

The non hairy skin found on our palms and soles is known as Glaborous skin. It has a thick epidermis layer with fingerprints.

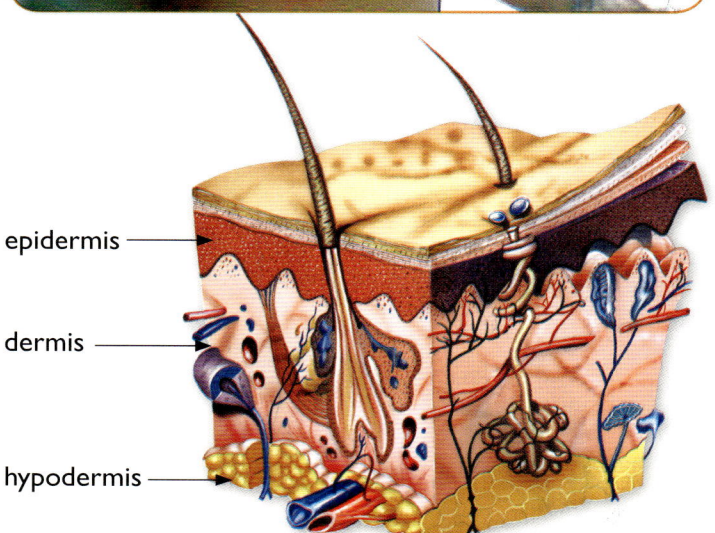
The thickness of the epidermis varies in different regions of the skin. It is 0.05 mm thick on the eyelids, and 1.5 mm thick on the palms and the soles of the feet.

Fair-skinned people have less melanin than dark-skinned people.

Skin Colour

The colour of our skin is determined by the amount and type of melanin. Melanin is a pigment produced by specialized cells called melanocytes. Albinism is an inherited disorder in which a child suffers with a total or partial lack of melanin in the skin.

Skin and Hair

Wrinkles

When a person ages, the epidermal cells become thinner and less elastic. This makes the skin sag and thus wrinkles appear. The number of epidermal cells decreases and they divide very slowly, making the skin incapable of repairing itself quickly.

Hair Growth

Hair are thread-like protein filaments. Hair grow from a cavity like structure called follicle. The base of the follicle is shaped like a bulb. Inside the bulb, new hair cells continuously form and push the hair out. Oil glands on the side of each follicle coat the growing hair and make it soft and supple.

Hair or No Hair

We have more follicles on the scalp and therefore more hair grow on our head. The soles of our feet, lips, and palms do not grow hair because they do not have hair follicles.

Hair Colour

The melanin found in the hair follicle determines our hair colour. Melanin is of two types—eumelanin and pheomelanin. Eumelanin is responsible for giving brown and black colour to the hair. As we grow old, our hair follicle stop making melanin and our hair turn gray.

The skin appears dry when wrinkles appear.

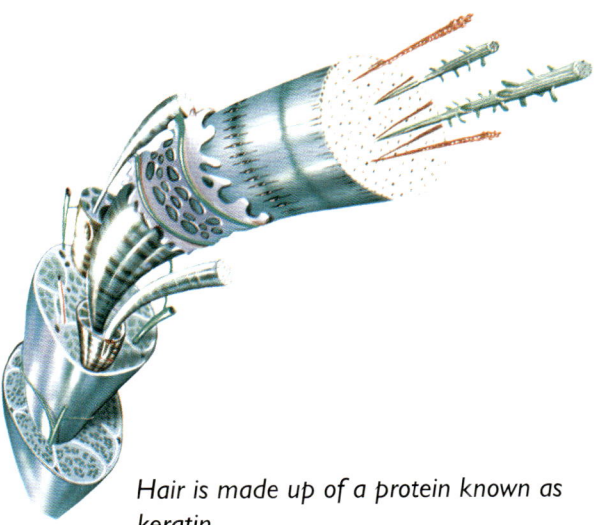

Hair is made up of a protein known as keratin

Pheomelanin is responsible for blond and red colour hair in humans.

HUMAN BODY

Muscle Fibers

Muscles are made up of muscle fibers. These fibers are joined together in bundles and are connected to the brain through the nerves. Nerves transmit signals from the brain to muscle fibers. The muscle fibers contract or relax accordingly.

Tendons and Ligaments

Muscles carry out all their movements with the help of tendons and ligaments. They are the joining tissues located at the joints. Tendons connect the muscles with the bones whereas ligaments connect bones together helping them to bend.

Bones – The Protective Frame

All bones in the body combine to form a protective framework called skeletal system. They provide support and structure to our body and also protect the delicate organs of body. For example, cranium protects our brain and vertebral column protects the spinal cord.

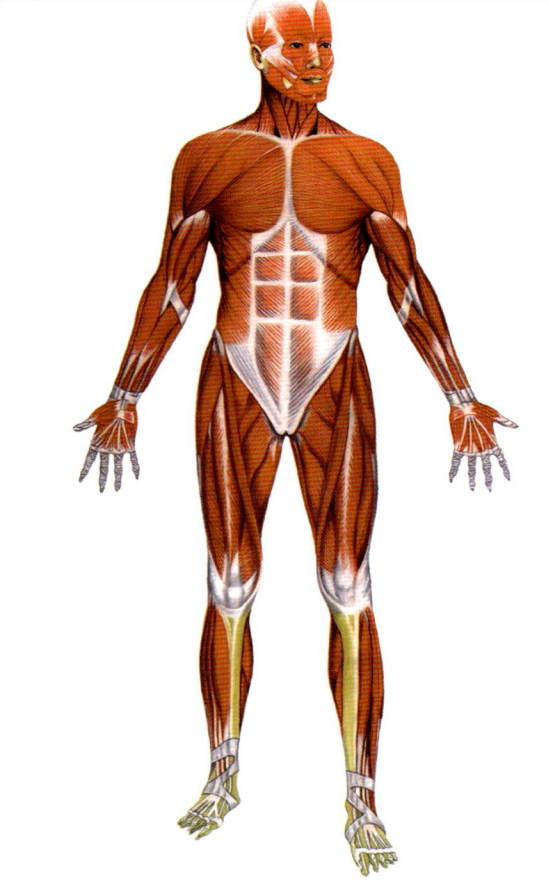

Thousands of long, thin fibers called muscle fibers make up the muscles.

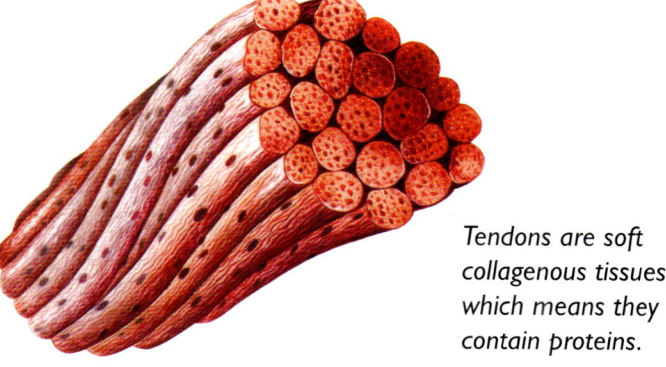

Tendons are soft collagenous tissues, which means they contain proteins.

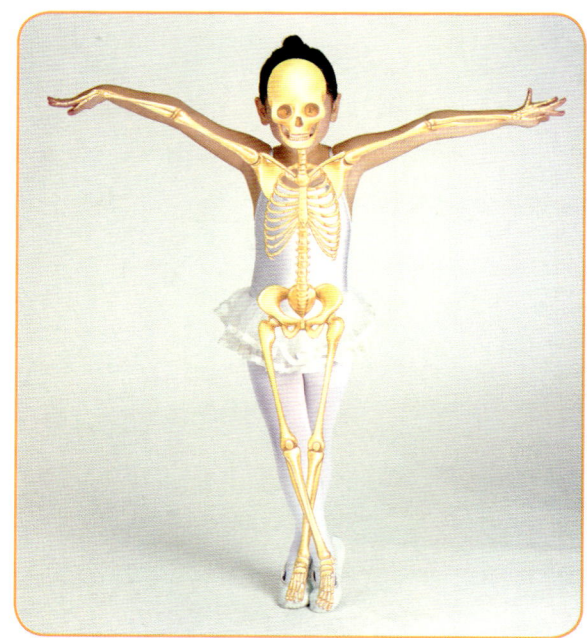

The skeletal system provides the framework and structure to the body.

Quick Look

Femur is the largest bone in our body that is found in the thigh.

Muscles, bones and joints

Types of Movable Joints

Ball and socket joint	-	hip and shoulder joint
Hinge joints	-	knee and elbow
Pivot joints	-	head
Ellipsoidal joint	-	index finger
Saddle joint	-	thumbs
Gliding joint	-	ankle and wrists

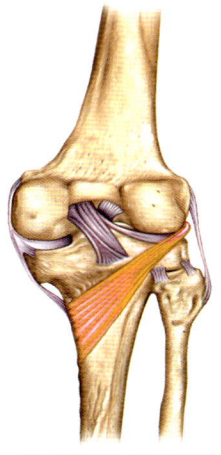

Bones provide flexibility and movement to our body.

Joints

Joints are the places where bones meet. Some joints are fixed and immovable; some are slightly movable, while others are completely movable. For example, skull is a fixed joint, spine and vertebrae are slightly movable joints.

Movable Joints

Movable joints are also called Synovial joints as these joints contain a fluid called synovial fluid between them. The synovial fluid allows the joint to move freely by decreasing friction.

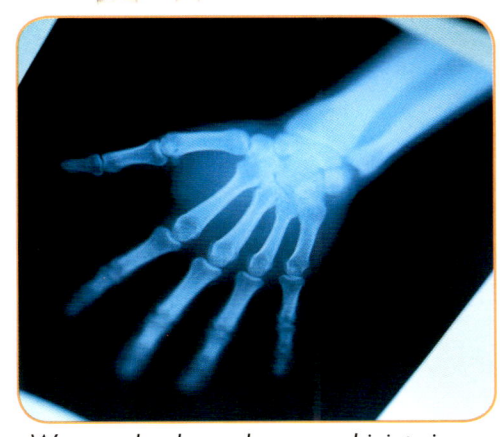

We can clearly see bones and joints in an X-ray film.

Types of Muscles

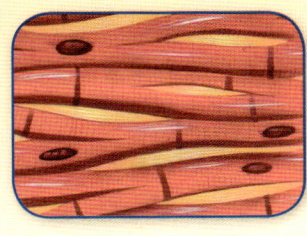

Cardiac muscles are found only in the heart helping it to pump properly and contracts involuntarily.

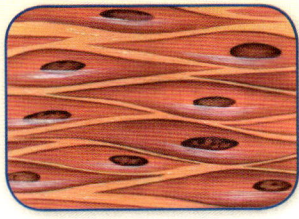

Smooth muscles are found in the digestive system, blood vessels, bladder, air tract and uterus. Smooth muscles are controlled by the nervous system. Therefore, they function involuntarily.

Skeletal muscles are attached to the skeleton and act voluntarily. A skeletal muscle links two bones across its connecting joint.

13

HUMAN BODY

Heart

Heart is a hollow muscular organ that pumps blood in the body. It receives impure blood from veins, and pumps pure blood into arteries. The heart has four chambers, the two top chambers are called atrium and the two bottom chambers are called ventricles. The left chambers are separated from the right chambers by a thick muscular wall known as septum.

Blood

Blood is made of red blood cells, white blood cells, and platelets. Blood cells float in a yellow-coloured liquid, called plasma. Blood carries oxygen and nutrients to all body parts and removes harmful wastes, such as carbon di-oxide, produced by the body. Platelets help in clotting of the blood.

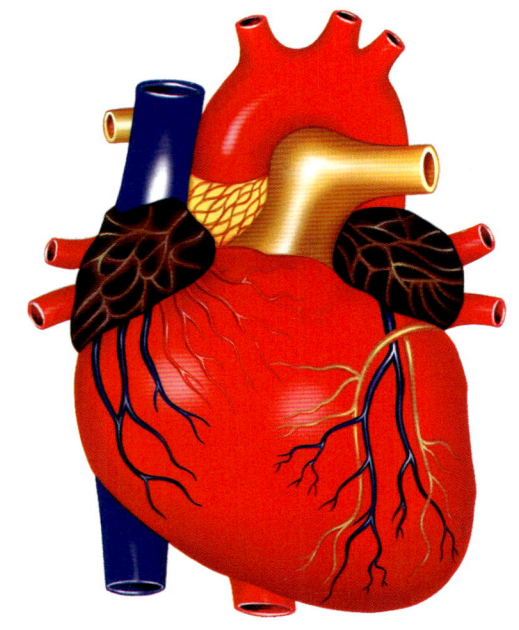

The human heart is the size of a closed fist, and weighs around 250 to 300 grams.

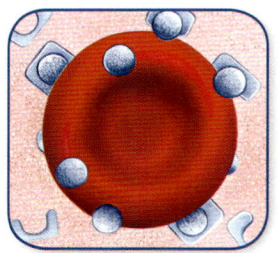

Blood gets its red colour from a pigment called hemoglobin, present in the red blood cells.

White blood cells fight against diseases and germs.

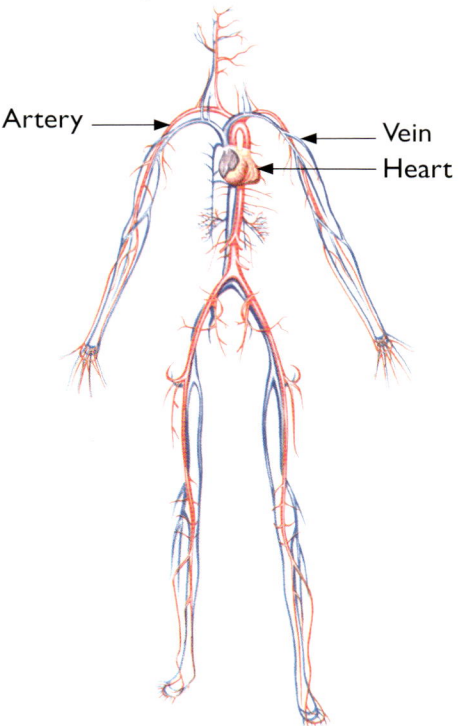

Blood reaches to all parts of the body through the circulatory system.

Blood Circulation

The right atrium receives deoxygenated blood from the body and sends it to the right ventricle. Right ventricle sends this blood to the lungs to become oxygen-rich. Oxygen-rich blood from the lungs moves to the left atrium and is then pumped into the left ventricle. The left ventricle contracts and sends this blood to the aorta that carries it throughout the body.

HEART AND BLOOD

Valves

Valves are four flap-like barriers in heart that control the blood flow between the chambers and when leaving the heart. Whenever these valves close, 'lub dub,' sounds are produced. The "lub" sound is produced when the tricuspid and mitral valves close. The "dub" sound is produced when the aortic and pulmonary valves close.

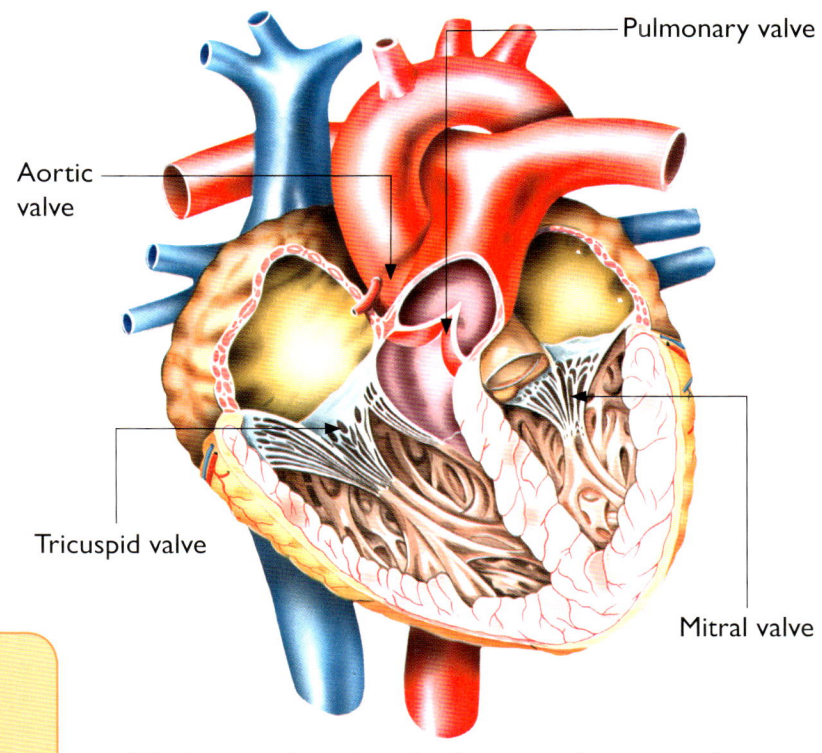

Mitral, tricuspid, aortic and pulmonary valves are the four valves in the heart.

Quick Look

Pulse is the rhythmic contraction and expansion of the arteries with each beat of the heart.

Systole Diastole

Contraction of the heart chambers when blood moves out of them is known as systole. Relaxation of the heart chambers, when they fill with blood is known as diastole.

Arteries and Veins

Arteries are blood vessels that carry blood away from the heart. Veins are blood vessels that carry blood to the heart. All arteries carry oxygenated blood except for pulmonary artery whereas all veins carry deoxygenated blood except for pulmonary vein.

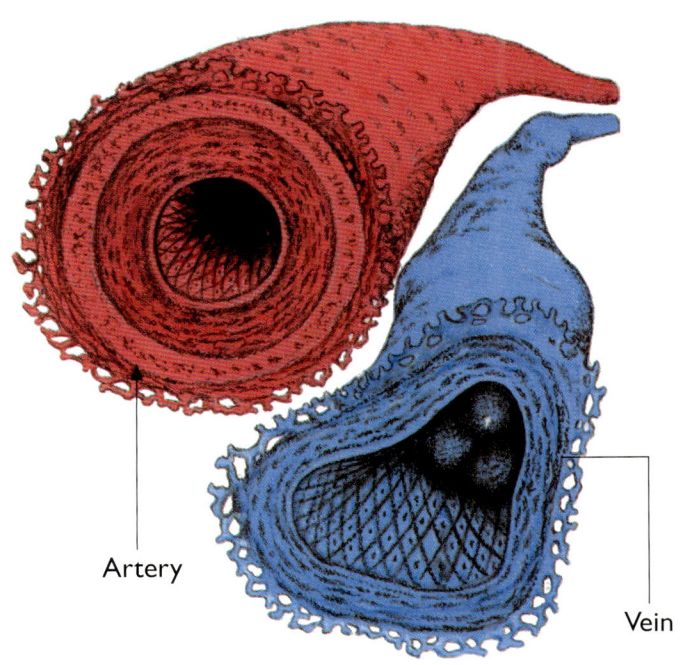

The aorta is the largest artery in the human body.

15

HUMAN BODY

Brain

Brain is a part of the central nervous system, located inside our head. Brain is made of three parts, cerebrum, cerebellum and brain stem. Our brain controls and coordinates the sense organs and bodily activities like body temperature, heart rate, breathing, blood pressure, etc.

Different Parts

Cerebrum is the largest part of the brain. It is covered by a thin sheet known as cerebral cortex. The major functions of the cerebrum include controlling thought process, voluntary movements, language and speech ability, reasoning power and perception.

Diencephalon

The central part of brain is the diencephalon. It includes thalamus, hypothalamus and epithalamus. Thalamus is made up of grey matter in the form of two oval-shaped masses. They are relay stations for sensory impulses. Hypothalamus controls the internal state of body with respect to the environment. Epithalamus acts like a biological clock controlling puberty and rhythmic cycles.

Brain Stem

Brain stem is the smallest part of the brain. The brain stem connects the brain to the spinal cord. It controls major body functions such as respiration, digestion, and blood circulation.

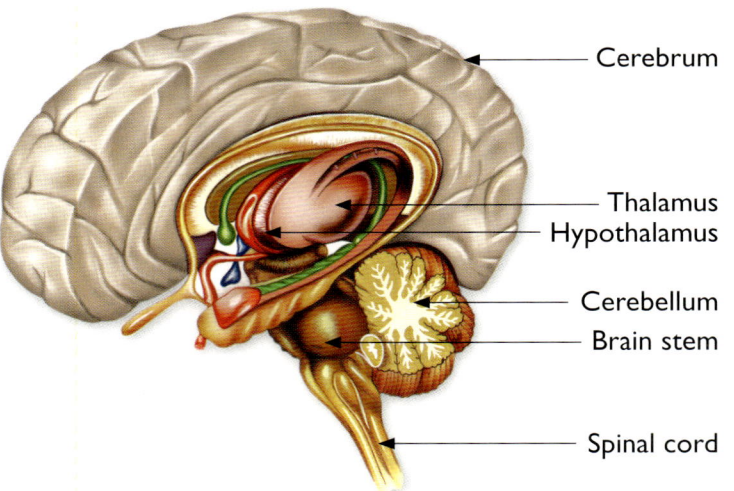

The cerebrum consists of the cortex, large fiber tracts (corpus callosum) and some deeper structures (basal ganglia, amygdala, and hippocampus).

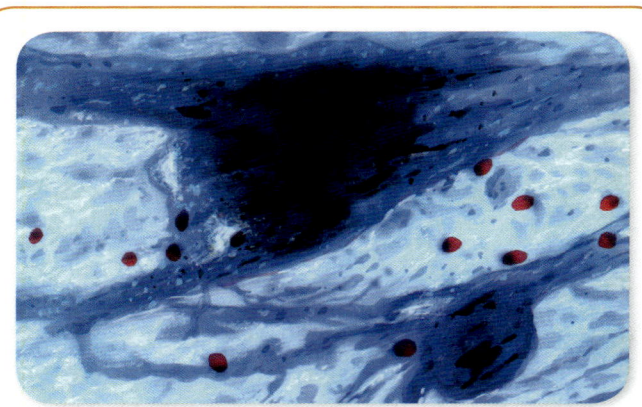

Nerve cells in spinal cord.

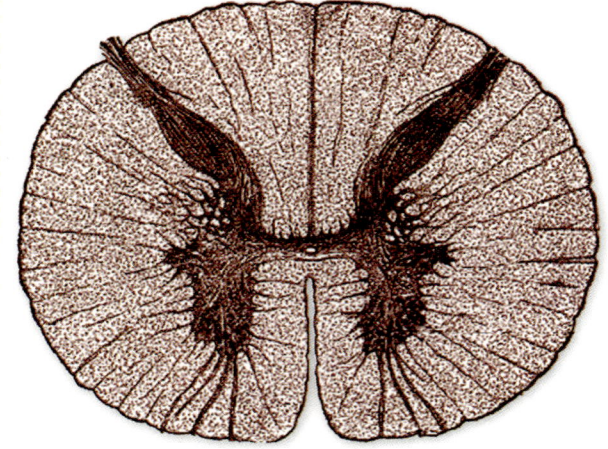

Spinal cord is a 46-cm-long structure of tissues that connects the brain with the rest of the body.

Brain and Nerves

Cerebellum

Cerebellum is located at the back of the brain. It is responsible for movement, control and balance of the body.

Nerves

Nerves are long bundles of nerve fibers. They carry information between the central nervous system and other organs of the body. Nerves are named according to the place of their origin. The nerves that originate from the brain are known as the cranial nerves. The nerves that originate from the spinal cord are known as the spinal nerves.

Spinal and Cranial Nerves

Thirty-one pairs of spinal nerves divide into 8 cervical nerves, 12 thoracic nerves, 5 lumbar nerves, 5 sacral nerves and 1 coccygeal nerve. There are 12 pairs of cranial nerves: olfactory, optic, oculomotor, trochlear, trigeminal, abducens, facial, vestibulocochlear, glossopharyngeal, vagus, accessory, and hypoglossal.

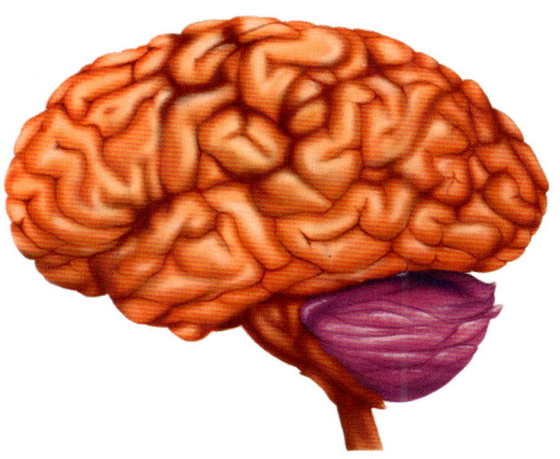

A human brain with the cerebellum in purple.

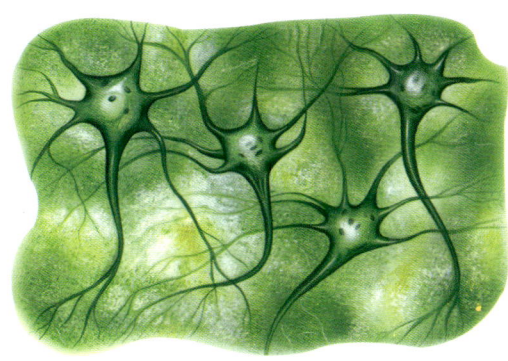

Cranial nerves are responsible for smell, vision, hearing, eye movements, facial expressions, chewing, taste, etc.

Quick Look

The scientific study of the brain and nervous system is called neuroscience or neurobiology.

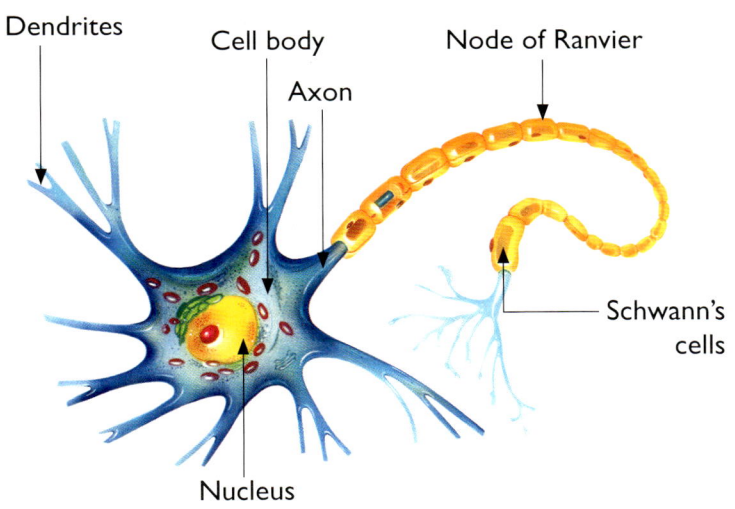

Cell body, axon and dendrites are the main components of a neuron.

Neurons

Nerves are made of millions of long and thin nerve cells known as neurons. Neurons are the basic structural and functional units of the nervous system. These neurons are connected to each other through branches coming out of them. There are about 30,000 million neurons in human body.

HUMAN BODY

Stomach

Stomach is a sac-like digestive organ located between the esophagus and the intestines. Stomach is the widest part of the digestive system that digests swallowed food flowing down from the esophagus. The food inside the stomach is churned into very small particles.

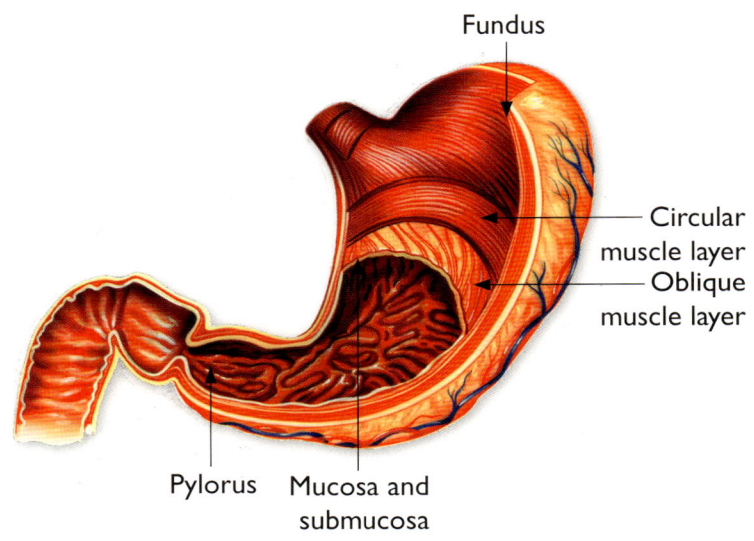

Mucosa and submucosa secrete gastric juices. The muscle layers contract and expand to mix and expel the contents in the stomach.

Digestive Juices and Enzymes

The stomach walls secrete digestive juices that contain enzymes. Enzymes break down food into smaller molecules that are easily absorbed by the body. For example, the stomach secretes enzyme pepsin that breaks down proteins, amylase that breaks down carbohydrates and lipase that breaks down fat. Our stomach secretes about 2 to 3 litres of gastric juice everyday.

A balanced diet contains all essential nutrients such as carbohydrates, proteins, fats and vitamins and minerals.

Absorption

Some of the useful substances from the food are absorbed by the muscle lining of the stomach. For further digestion, the food, in form of a thick liquid called chyme, moves from the stomach into the small intestines.

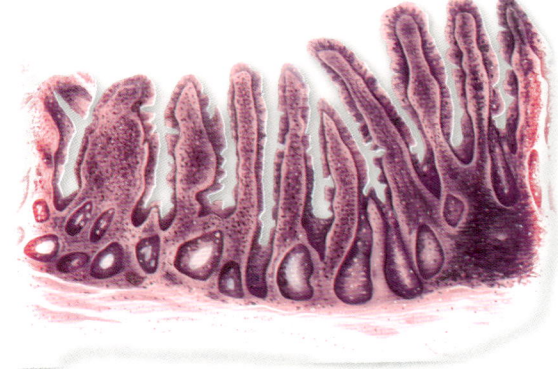

Villi are tiny, finger-like projections on the surface of the small intestine that help to absorb nutrients.

Quick Look

If stretched out, our small intestine would be about seven metres long.

Stomach And Intestines

Small Intestines

Semi-liquid food from stomach moves into the small intestine, where digestion of food continues and nutrients such as vitamins, fats, proteins are absorbed. The inner wall of the small intestine consists of millions of microscopic, finger-like projections called villi. Villi helps in the absorption of nutrients into the body. The small intestine is divided into 3 sections- duodenum, jejunum and ileum.

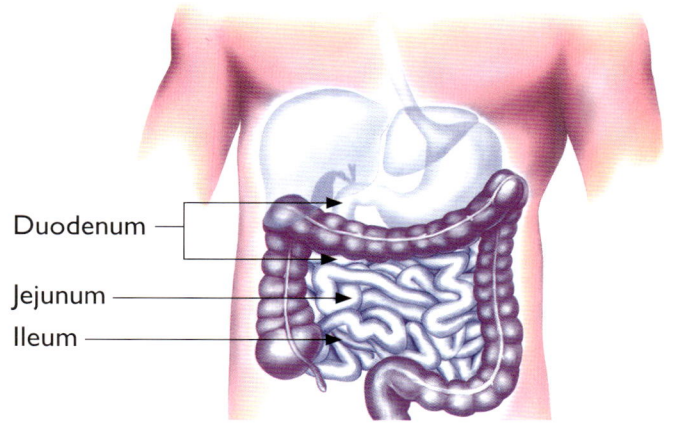

The lining of the small intestine secretes a hormone called secretin, which stimulates the pancreas to produce digestive enzymes.

Large Intestines

The large intestine is about 1.5 meters long. It is in the large intestines that waste products from the digested food are collected and processed for excretion. Water and certain vitamins are also reabsorbed in the large intestine.

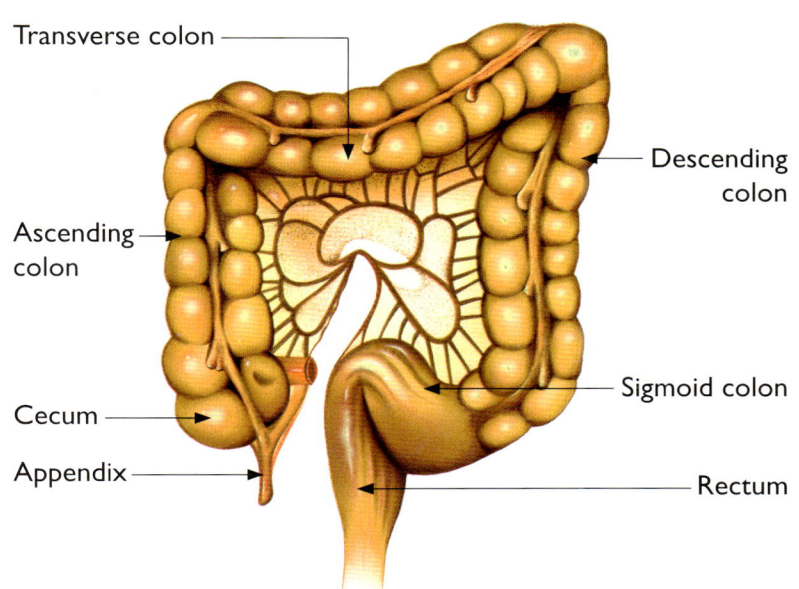

The large intestine is divided into 6 parts: cecum, ascending colon, transverse colon, descending colon, sigmoid colon and rectum.

Dyspepsia

Malfunctioning of the stomach or small intestines causes acid reflux. Acid reflux is a condition when the stomach acid backs up in our food pipe. This disorder is known as dyspepsia or indigestion. Indigestion leads to burning pain in the upper abdomen and chest. It can be cured by taking antacids that neutralize acid or help to stop the stomach acids flowing back.

Indigestion can be prevented by taking regular meals and a balanced diet.

HUMAN BODY

Digestive Organs

Liver and pancreas are important digestive organs. Liver is the largest internal organ of our body and is located above the stomach. Pancreas is a small, comma-shaped gland located behind the stomach. Both liver and pancreas play an important role in digestion of food and regulation of body's metabolism.

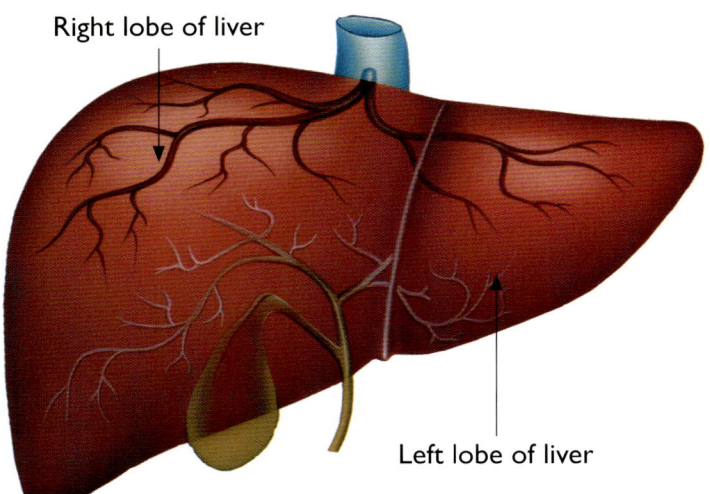

Liver plays an important role in digestion of food.

Blood Flow in Liver

Blood is carried to the liver by two large vessels called the hepatic artery and the portal vein. The hepatic artery carries oxygen-rich blood from the aorta to the liver. The portal vein carries blood containing digested food from the small intestine to the liver.

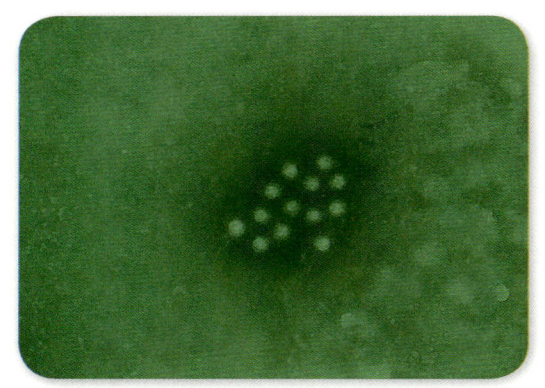

Hepatitis is a liver disease caused by a virus.

Liver Functions

The liver has many functions. Liver produces a digestive substance known as bile that breaks down fats. Liver stores glucose in the form of glycogen and releases it at the time of quick energy requirement. Liver is also responsible for making cholesterol that is important for the growth of cells and hormones. It also produces waste products like urea.

Quick Look

The liver filters more than a liter of blood each minute.

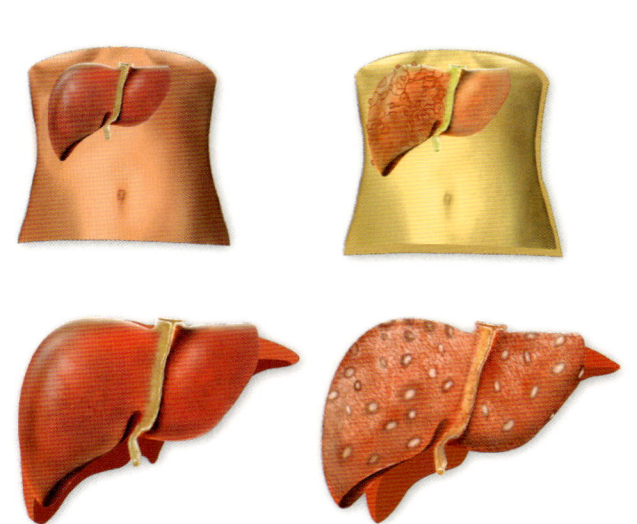

Healthy liver   Cirrhosis of the liver

In liver cirrhosis, normal liver tissues are destroyed and the liver shrinks and is filled with fibrous tissues.

LIVER AND PANCREAS

Pancreas' Functions

Pancreas secretes enzymes that help in digestion. The enzymes secreted by pancreas flow into the small intestines where they help in the break down of fats, proteins and carbohydrates. Pancreas also releases hormones. Insulin and glucagon are the two main hormones produced by the pancreas. These two hormones regulate the blood sugar level in the body.

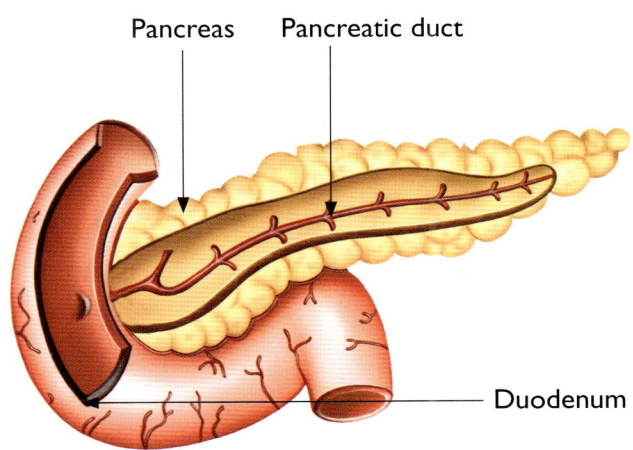

Pancreas secretes enzymes and hormones that help in digestion of food.

Pancreatitis

Pancreatitis is a disease caused by the inflammation of the pancreas. There are two forms of pancreatitis - acute pancreatitis and chronic pancreatitis. The two disorders are different in causes and symptoms, and require different treatment. Acute pancreatitis is a rapidly-onset inflammation of the pancreas, most frequently caused by consuming too much alcohol or by the presence of gallstones. Chronic pancreatitis is a long-standing inflammation of the pancreas.

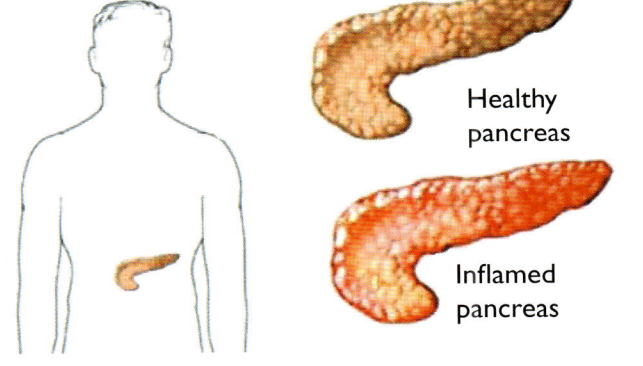

Pancreatitis is caused by the digestion of the tissues of the pancreas by its own enzymes.

Jaundice

Jaundice is caused when the liver functions improperly. The liver normally removes a toxic pigment called bilirubin from blood. In the case of jaundice, liver is unable to remove this pigment and thus its amount increases in the body causing the symptoms of jaundice.

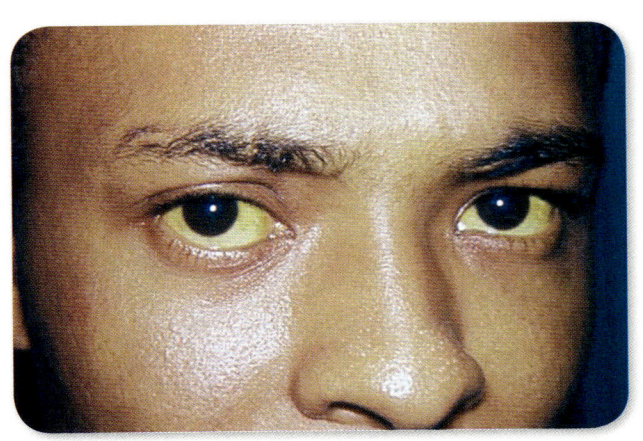

Yellowing of skin, eyes, and urine, nausea, fever and weakness are the major symptoms of jaundice.

HUMAN BODY

Lungs

Lungs are two triangular-shaped organs located inside our chest. They are the main respiratory organs, which supply oxygen to the blood in exchange of carbon di-oxide. Lungs are protected by rib cage and are covered with a membrane known as pulmonary pleura.

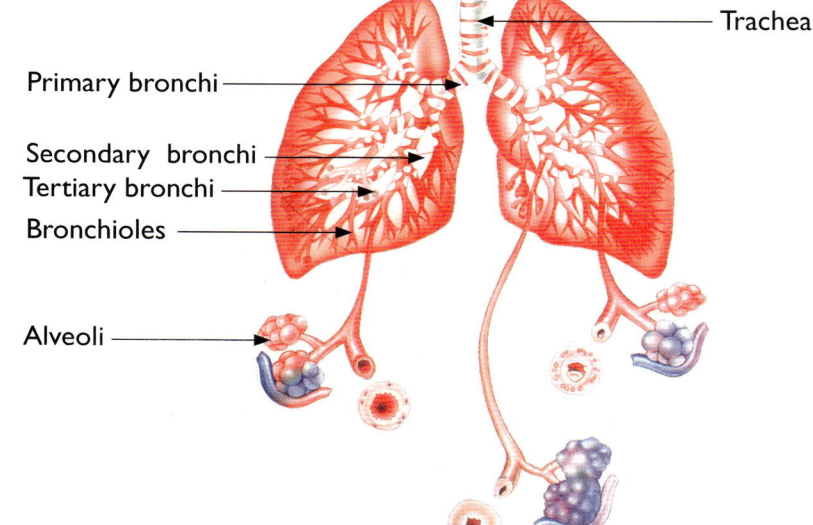

The left lung is slightly smaller than the right lung.

Breathing

The bodily process of inhalation and exhalation is called breathing. The process of taking air into the lungs is called inhalation, and the process of breathing it out is called exhalation.

Trachea and Bronchi

The oxygen that we inhale passes through the trachea, the wind pipe connecting mouth and nose to lungs. In the chest cavity, the trachea splits into two smaller tubes called the bronchi that enter each lung.

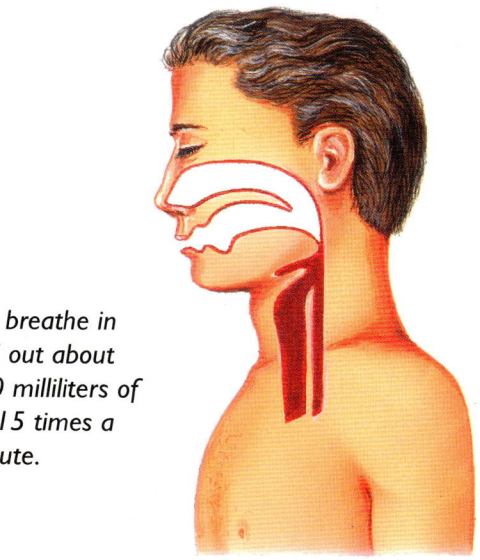

We breathe in and out about 500 milliliters of air 15 times a minute.

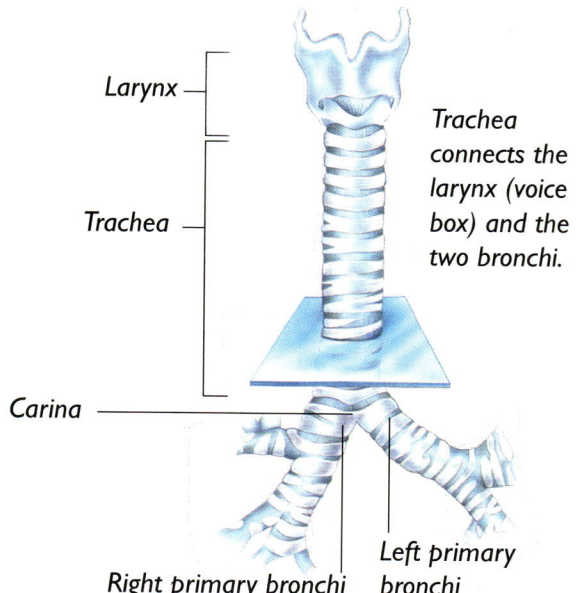

Trachea connects the larynx (voice box) and the two bronchi.

Bronchial Tube and Alveoli

Inside each lung, a bronchus spreads in a tree-like fashion into smaller tubes called bronchial tube, which further ends in a tiny sac-like air chamber known as alveolus. The oxygen travels through all these parts and finally reaches the alveoli.

Quick Look

On the way down the windpipe, there are tiny hair called cilia that move gently to keep mucus and dirt out of the lungs.

Lungs and Breathing

Site of Gas Exchange

Alveoli are the main site of gas exchange. Alveoli are surrounded by blood capillaries. The carbon di-oxide-rich blood from the veins is released in the blood capillaries. This carbon di-oxide is taken away by the alveoli and is exhaled out of the lungs. The inhaled oxygen is transferred from alveoli to the blood in capillaries. Capillaries transfer this oxygenated blood to the arteries that distribute it to all body parts.

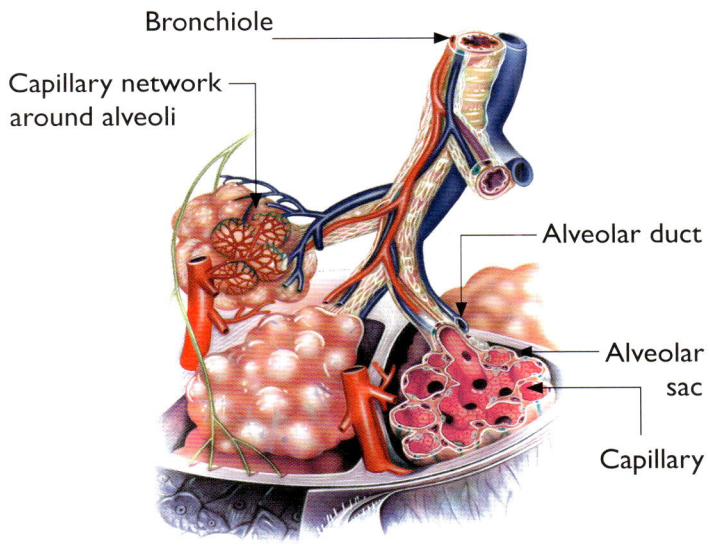

The average adult's lungs contain about 600 million alveoli.

Asthma

Asthma is a respiratory disease that occurs due to swelling of the air passage leading to less air flow in lungs. Its symptoms are wheezing, coughing, chest tightness, and troubled breathing. An asthma attack is a reaction to a trigger, a substance that initiates asthma. Asthma triggers can range from viruses (such as colds) to allergies, to gases and particles in the air.

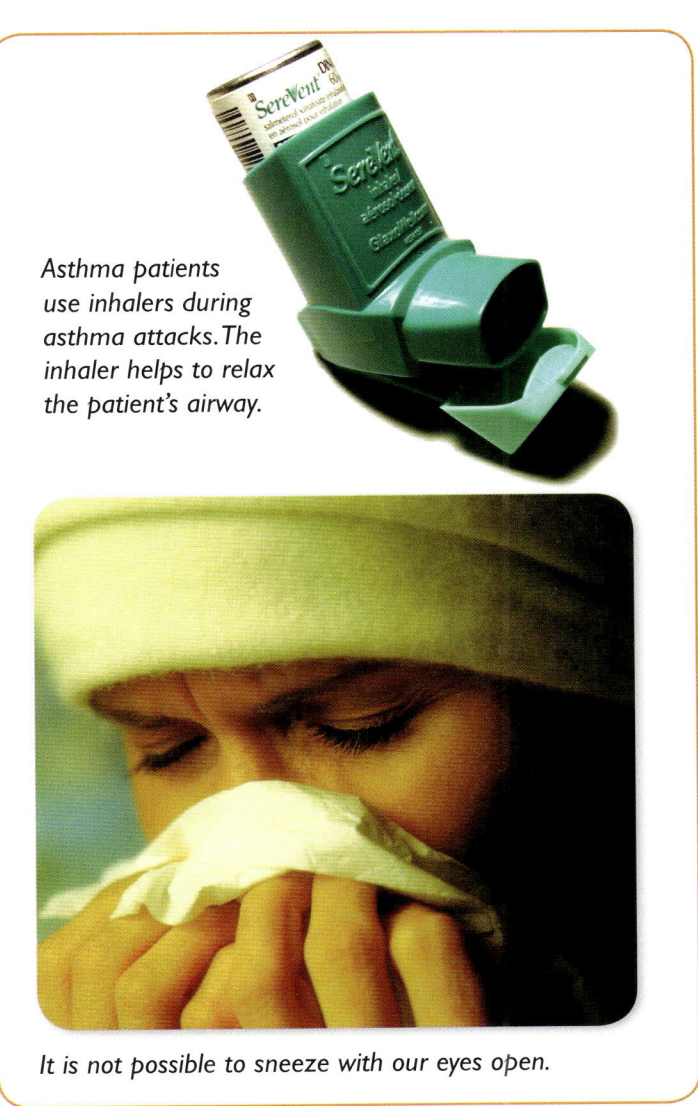

Asthma patients use inhalers during asthma attacks. The inhaler helps to relax the patient's airway.

Coughing and Sneezing

Pollen, dust and other harmful pollutants in the inhaled air are detected by specialized nerve cells present in our breathing pathway. The respiratory system responds to these substances by coughing and sneezing that result in expulsion of air, which clears the breathing pathway.

It is not possible to sneeze with our eyes open.

HUMAN BODY

Kidney

Kidneys are two bean-shaped organs located at the back side of our abdomen. They are the main excretory organs that filter out excess fluids and wastes, like urea, from the blood. A normal kidney measures about 10 centimeters long and 5 centimetres thick.

Filtration

Blood enters the kidney and passes into nephrons. Nephrons separate urea, mineral salts, and toxins from the blood. The waste fluid, known as urine, is passed through ureter to urinary bladder. Urinary bladder releases this fluid out of the body.

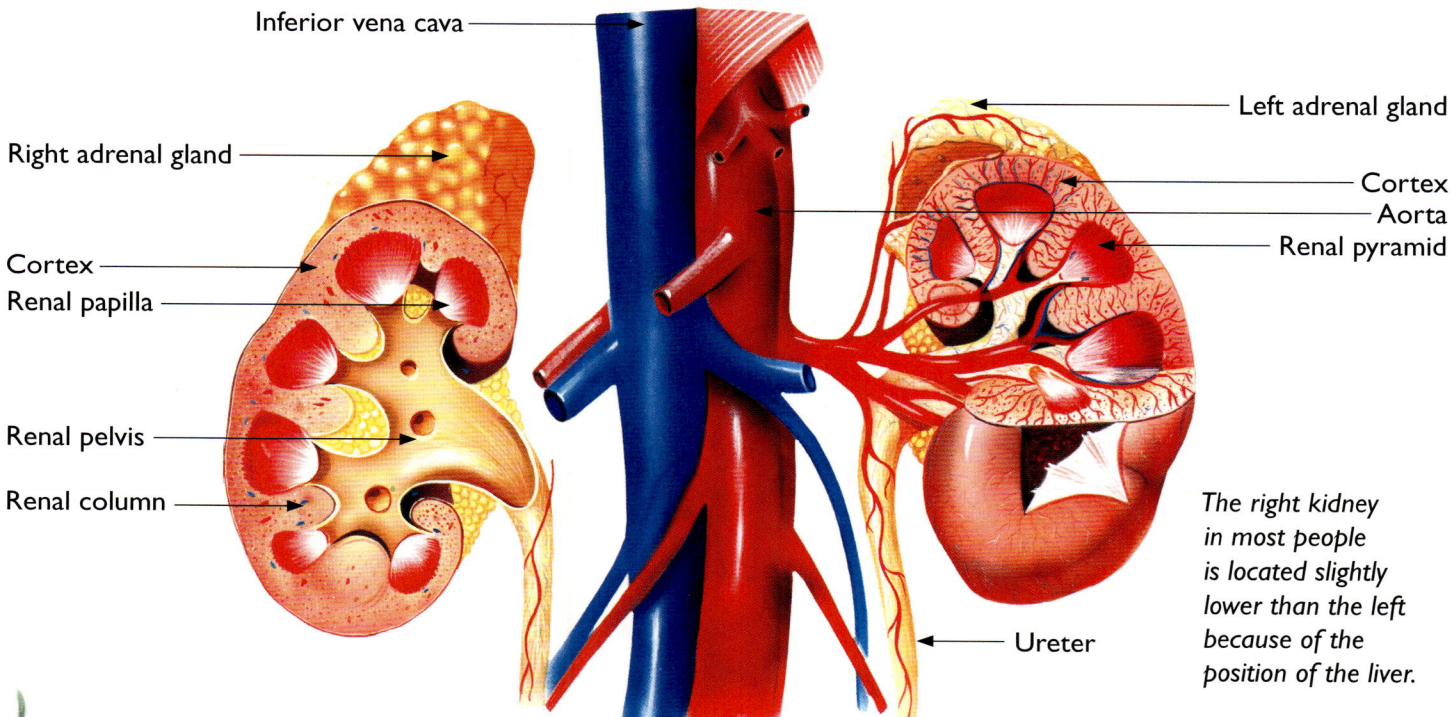

The right kidney in most people is located slightly lower than the left because of the position of the liver.

Homeostasis

Kidneys play an important role in balancing the volume of fluids and minerals in the body. This balance in the body is called homeostasis.

Nephrons

There are over one million tiny tubes inside the kidneys. These tubes are called nephrons. Nephrons are the basic functional and structural units of kidney. Nephrons function as filters and are responsible for the purification of blood.

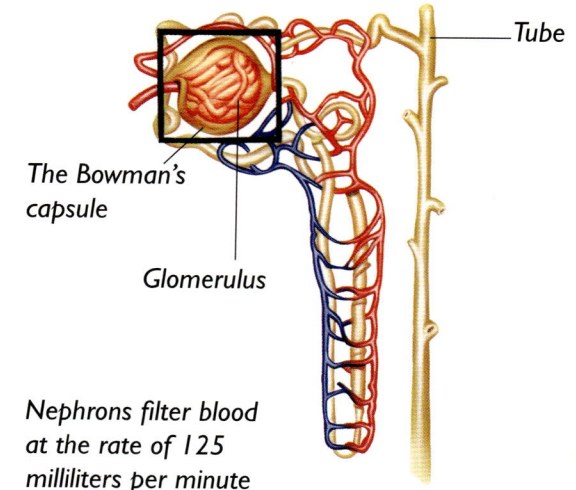

Nephrons filter blood at the rate of 125 milliliters per minute

Kidneys and Nephrons

Parts of Nephron

Each nephron consists of a tiny cluster of blood vessels called a glomerulus. Glomerulus is surrounded by a cup-like structure known as the Bowman's capsule. As blood flows through the glomerulus, water, salts and wastes pass into the Bowman's capsule. Then these wastes ooze into a U-shaped tube, called the loop of Henle. The loop of Henle reabsorbs useful salts, minerals and some water from the filtered blood.

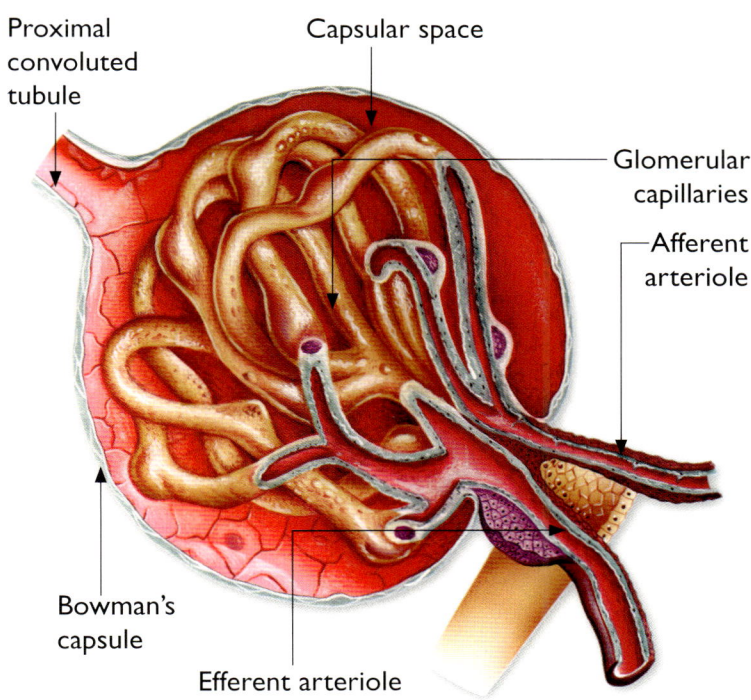

Inflammation of the capillary loops in the glomeruli is called glomerulonephritis. In this condition, the kidneys are unable to filter waste products from the blood.

Nephritis

Nephritis is inflammation of kidneys. It can be caused by disorder in immune response. When the kidneys inflame, they excrete out the needed protein from the body, leading to a condition called proteinuria. Proteins prevent blood from clotting, so in deficiency of proteins many blood clots can form causing sudden stroke. Nephritis results in water retention that causes swelling of hands and feet.

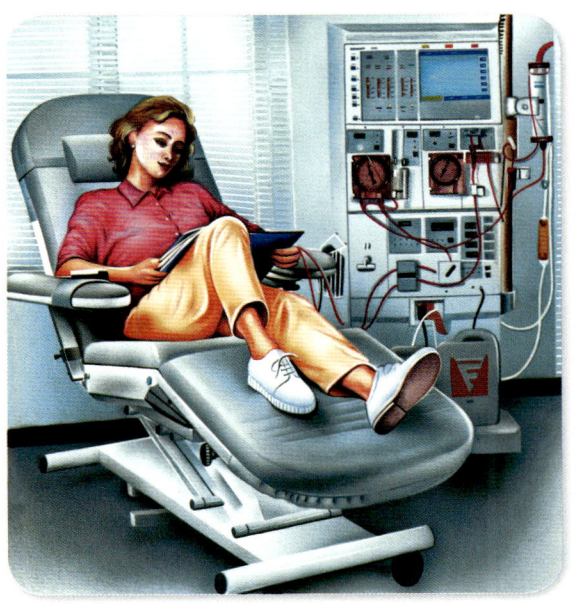

A patient undergoing dialysis.

Hormone Release

Kidneys produce a hormone known as erythropoietin. Erythropoietin stimulates production of red cells in the bone marrow. In case of a kidney disease, production of this hormone can decline and can cause anemia.

Quick Look

Dialysis is a medical treatment for dysfunctional kidneys in which toxins are removed from the blood using machines and equipments.

HUMAN BODY

What is reproduction?

Reproduction is a biological process by which organisms produce offspring. Two kinds of sex cells or gametes play a role in human reproduction. The male gamete or sperm fertilises the female gamete or ovum.

Fertilisation

Fertilisation takes place when the sperm fertilises the female ovum or egg. Fertilisation occurs in the fallopian tube. After fertilisation, a zygote is formed. A zygote contains 50% genes from the sperm and 50% from the egg. The zygote attaches itself to the wall of the uterus and develops into an embryo. This embryo grows and develops into a baby.

Ovulation

Ovulation is the cyclic production of an egg and its release from the ovary. The egg is produced in the ovary and released into a fallopian tube.

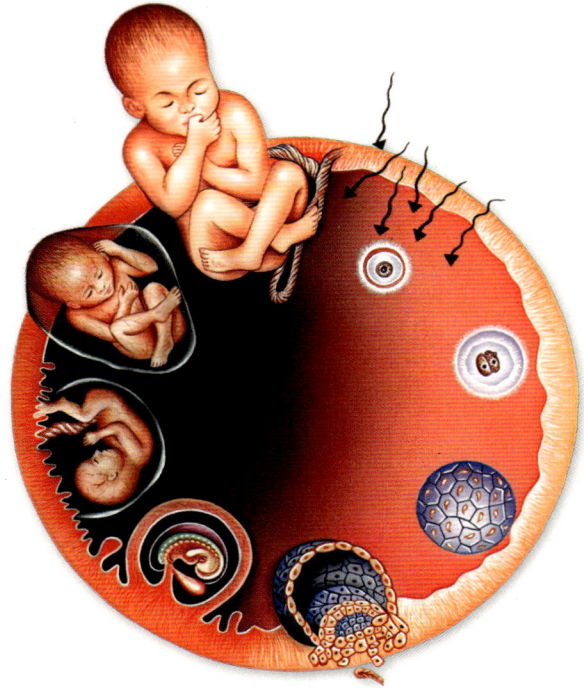

Development of a zygote into a baby.

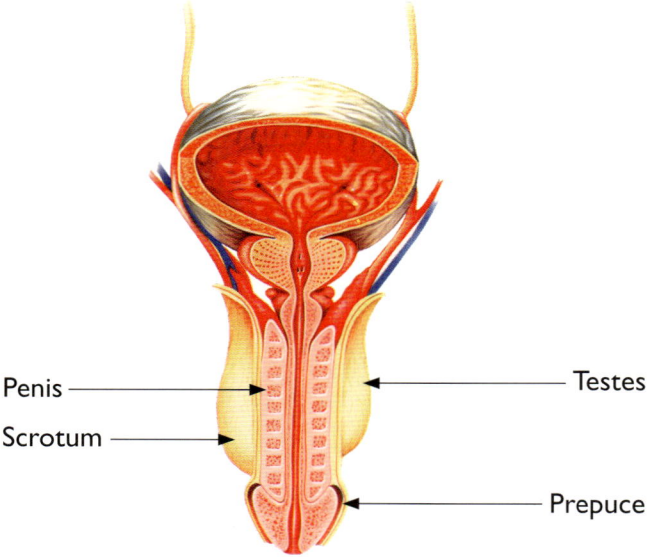

The testis lie directly behind the penis and is situated outside the body in the scrotum.

Quick Look

The lifespan of a sperm is about 36 hours, while the lifespan of an ovum is 12 to 24 hours.

Male Reproductive Organs

- Testicles
- Duct system consisting of the epididymis and vas deferens
- Accessory glands, which include the seminal vesicles and prostate gland
- Penis

Female Reproductive Organs

- Ovaries, which produce eggs
- Fallopian tubes
- Uterus or the womb supports and nourishes the fetus during pregnancy
- Vagina

Reproduction

Ovaries and Fallopian Tubes

Ovaries and fallopian tubes are parts of female reproductive system. Ovaries are two oval-shaped organs located on either side of the uterus. Fallopian tubes are two tubes, each attached to a side of the uterus.

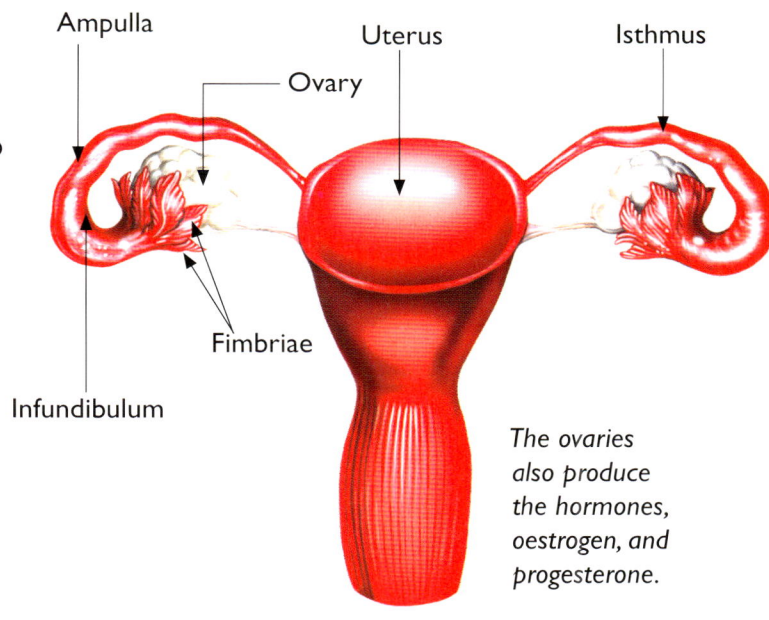

Testicles and Duct System

Testicles, epididymis and vas deferens are the main reproductive organs in males. The testicles are two oval-shaped organs that produce and store millions of tiny sperm cells. The epididymis is a set of coiled tubes that connects to the vas deferens. Epididymis and vas deferens make up the duct system.

The ovaries also produce the hormones, oestrogen, and progesterone.

Pregnancy

Pregnancy is the period between the fertilization of the egg and the birth of the baby. A normal pregnancy lasts for about 40 weeks or 9 months. Pregnancy is divided into the three trimesters.

Childbirth happens after nine months.

Trimester	First			Second			Third		
Month	one	two	three	four	five	six	seven	eight	nine
Weeks	1–4	5–8	9–13	14–17	18–21	22–26	27–30	31–35	36–40

A child shares the same genes as his or her's parents; therefore the child resembles her parents. Genes are the units of genetic information that are passed from parent to offspring and found on chromosomes in the nucleus of each cell. Humans have 23 pairs of chromosomes. Both the parents contribute one of each pair of chromosomes.

HUMAN BODY

What is First Aid?

First aid is an emergency or immediate treatment given to an injured, wounded, or sick person. It generally consists of a series of simple, life-saving techniques until professional medical treatment can be provided.

First Aid Kit

A first-aid kit is a standard collection of supplies and equipment for giving first aid. First aid kits can be purchased commercially, or can be made at home.

It is important to carry first-aid kits in vehicles as they may be required in case of an accident.

Inside a First Aid Kit

- Disposable gloves
- Pack of cotton
- Bandages – elastic bandages, gauze roller bandages, adhesive elastic roller bandages, adhesive bandages, and sterile dressings
- Pads – sterile eye pads and gauze pads
- Instruments – scissors, tweezers, needle, thermometer, emergency blanket, penlight, and syringe
- Creams and gels – burn gels, antiseptic cream, antibiotic and anesthetic ointment or spray
- Tablets and solutions – painkillers and ORS sachet

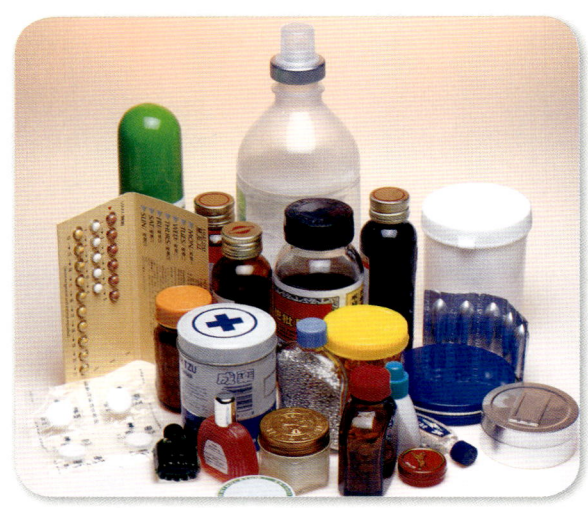

A first-aid kit contains medicines, ointments and bandages.

Conditions that Often Require First Aid

- Bleeding
- Bruise
- Eye injury
- Poisoning
- Animal bite
- Insect sting
- Burn
- Chemical burn
- Sunburn
- Electrical shock
- Choking
- Infant Choking
- Unconsciousness

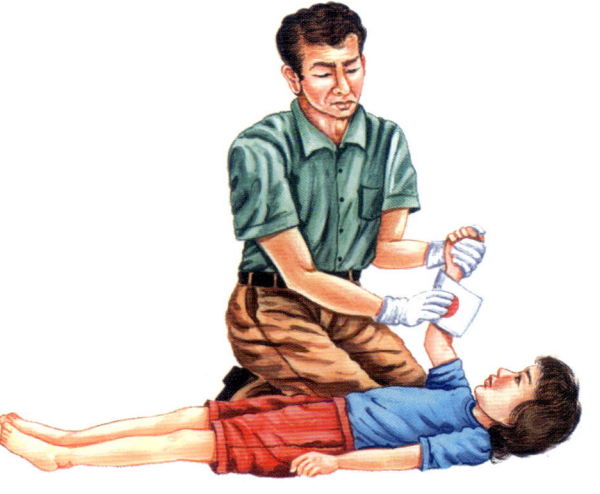

First aid for a bleeding arm.

FIRST AID

First Aid – What Not to Do

1. Do not put butter or cream on a burn. Put cold water.
2. Only an X-ray can determine a broken limb. Even if you can move a limb, it may be broken.
3. Do not put a wound under a tap to stop bleeding. It washes away the body's clotting agents and makes it bleed more.
4. Do not treat nosebleeds by putting the head back. If you put the head back, all the blood goes down the back of the airway.
5. Do not use a tourniquet to treat serious bleeding. It's harmful to stop the blood flow to a limb for more than 10-15 minutes.
6. Do not make a person puke when she has swallowed poison. The vomit may block the airway.
7. Do not perform CPR (cardiopulmonary resuscitation) on someone who has a pulse. It can damage their heart.

First Aid – Infant Choking

1. Call for medical help.
2. Place the infant's face down on the forearm. Support the head and neck with the hand.
3. Rest your hand on your knee with the infant's head lower than her body.
4. With the heel of your hand, give four blows between the infant's shoulder blades.
5. Turn the infant over.
6. Place two fingers just below the nipples, on the center of the infant's chest and perform up to five chest thrusts.
7. Repeat until obstruction is clear.

A man helping a choking child expel the foreign body out of her mouth.

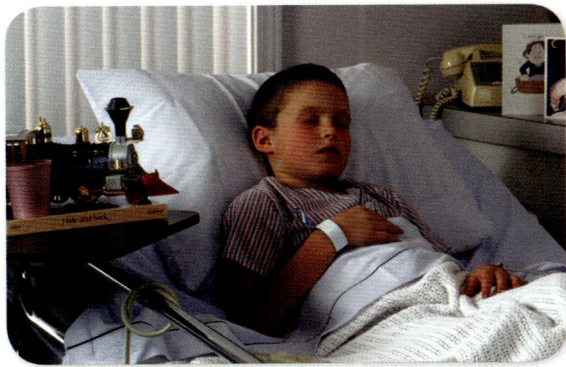

Some patients may need to be hospitalised even after being given first aid.

Quick Look

A blocked airway can kill a person in 3 to 4 minutes. A simple first aid procedure such as opening the airway can save a life.

First Aid – Insect Bites

1. Ask the patient not to move the limb.
2. Apply a tight bandage above the bite mark (towards heart).
3. If the person is unconscious, call for an ambulance.

First Aid – Dog Bite

1. Wipe away the saliva from the wound.
2. Wash the wound with water and soap.
3. Shift the patient to a hospital.

HUMAN BODY

Bacterial Diseases

Bacteria are single-celled microscopic organisms that cause bacterial diseases in humans. Bacteria that cause diseases are called pathogenic bacteria. They enter the human body through contaminated food, water or through close contact with an infected person.

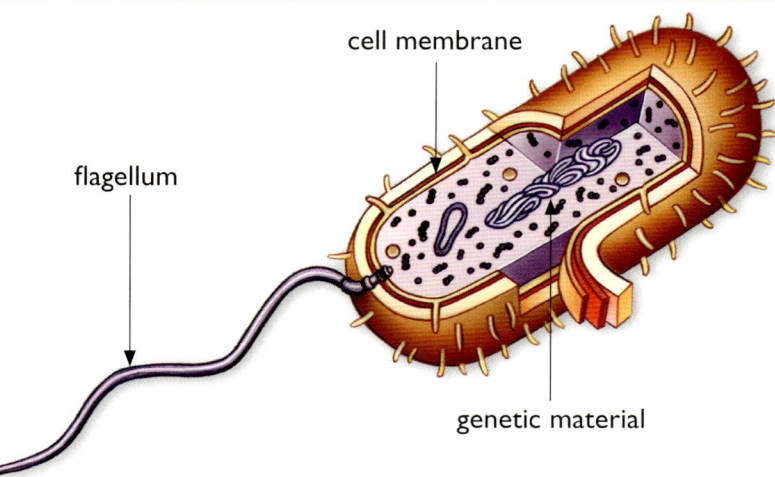

A typical bacterium.

Bacterial Diseases

Name	Caused by
Diphtheria	Corynebacterium diphtheriae
Gonorrhea	Neisseria gonorrhoeae
Tuberculosis	Mycobacterium tuberculosis
Acne	Propionibacterium acnes
Inhalation Anthrax	Bacillus anthracis
Pneumonia	Streptococcus pneumoniae, Chlamydophila pneumoniae, Haemophilus influenzae
Leprosy	Mycobacterium leprae
Cholera	Vibrio cholerae
Typhoid fever	Salmonella typhi

Viral Diseases

Name	Caused by
Smallpox	Variola
Measles	Rubeola
Common Cold	Corona virus
Hepatitis	Hepadnavirus-B, Picornavirus-A
Mumps	Paramyxovirus
Chickenpox	Herpes varicella zoster

Quick Look

Antibiotics are drugs that kill bacteria and other disease causing organisms. Antibiotics are produced from microorganisms.

Genetic Diseases

Name	Caused by
Sickle cell anemia	hemoglobin or HBB gene
Down syndrome	extra 21st chromosome
Cystic fibrosis	CFTR gene
Hemophilia A	FVIII gene
Hemophilia B	FIX gene
Muscular dystrophy	Collagen Type VI
Colour blindness	X-linked recessive gene

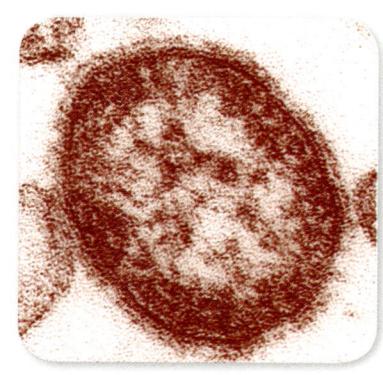

Measles is a highly contagious viral disease. Measles virus is transmitted to people when they come in contact with fluids from an infected person's nose and mouth.

FIGHTING DISEASES

Types of Cancers

1. Breast and ovarian cancer
2. Burkitt lymphoma
3. Colon cancer
4. Harvey Ras oncogene
5. Leukemia, chronic myeloid
6. Lung carcinoma, small cell
7. Malignant melanoma
8. Multiple endocrine neoplasia
9. Neurofibromatosis
10. Pancreatic cancer
11. Polycystic kidney disease
12. Prostate cancer
13. Retinoblastoma
14. The p53 tumor suppressor protein
15. Tuberous sclerosis
16. Von Hippel-Lindau syndrome

Treatment of Cancer

Cancer treatment methods include chemotherapy, immunotherapy and radiation therapy. Chemotherapy uses drug or a combination of drugs to kill cancer cells. Immunotherapy boosts the body's own immune system to attack and destroy cancerous cells. Radiation therapy uses x-rays to kill cancer cells and shrink tumors.

Viral Diseases

Viruses cause viral diseases in humans. Viruses reproduce only after entering a living cell. Viruses spread from one person to another through coughs, sneezes, vomits or contact with body fluid of an infected person.

HIV

HIV is a retrovirus that causes AIDS. HIV attacks the immune system. There are two types of HIV – HIV-1 and HIV-2. HIV-1 is easily transmitted and causes most of the HIV infections. There is no cure or vaccine for HIV or AIDS.

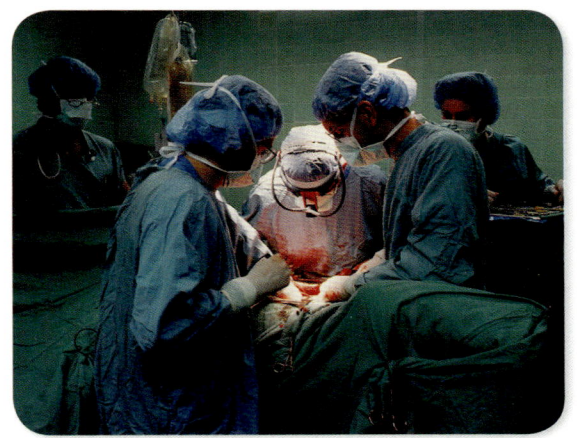

Many a times, the cancerous growth is removed by surgery.

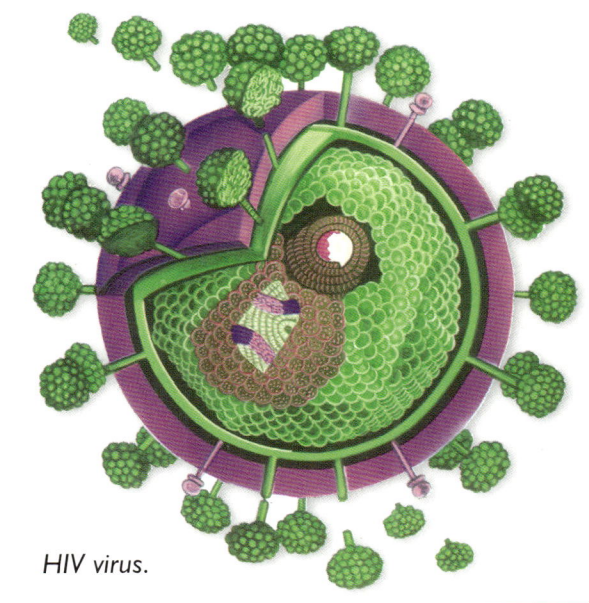

HIV virus.

HUMAN BODY

Index

A
amylase 18
anesthetic 28
antacids 19
atrium 14

B
bilirubin 21
biological 3, 16, 26
blanket 28
bone marrow 25
bruise 28

C
carbohydrate 3
cartilages 8
cell membrane 4
choking 28-29
cholesterol 20
choroid 6
chyme 18
cilia 22
conjunctiva 6
connective tissue 5
cornea 6
cranium 12
crown 9
cytoplasm 4

D
dentine 9
dermis 10
dialysis 25
duodenum 19

E
ear canal 7
eardrum 7
enamel 8, 9
enzyme 18
epidermis 10
epithelial tissue 5
erythropoietin 25
esophagus 18
eumelanin 11
excretion 19
eyesight 3

F
fats 3
femur 12
follicles 10-11

G
glaborous skin 10
glomerulus 25
glucagon 21
gonorrhea 30

H
hepatic artery 20
Hepatitis 20, 30
hypodermis 10

I
ileum 19
inhalation Anthrax 30
insulin 21
iris 6

J
jejunum 19

L
lachrymal glands 7
leprosy 30
loop of Henle 25

M
measles 30
meiosis 4
melanin 10-11
microscope 4
microscopic 19, 30
mitral valves 15
mucus membrane 6
mumps 30
muscle cells 4
muscle tissue 5
myopia 7

N
nerve cells 4, 8, 17, 23
neuroscience 17
nostrils 8
nucleus 4
nutrients 2-3, 14, 19

O
ointment 28
ossicles 7
ovary 26
oxygen 2, 5, 14, 20, 22

P
paramyxovirus 30
pathogenic bacteria 30
penlight 28
pepsin 18
pheomelanin 11
portal vein 20
protein 3
proteinuria 25
pulmonary pleura 22
pulmonary valves 15
pulse 15
pupil 6

R
retina 6
rubeola 30

S
saliva 29
sclera 6
septum 8, 14
skull 13
smallpox 30
sperm 26-27
spine 13
syringe 28

T
thermometer 28
tricuspid 15

U
unconsciousness 28
uterus 13, 26-27

V
variola 30
ventricles 14
vibrations 7
villi 19
vitamins 3

W
wrinkles 3, 11

Z
zygote 26-27

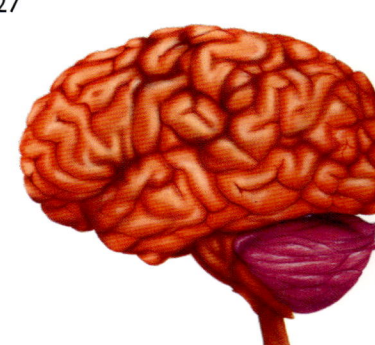